KT-572-674

21ST
CENTURY
DEBATES

WORLD
HEALTH

THE IMPACT ON OUR LIVES

DR RONAN FOLEY

HODDER
Wayland

an imprint of Hodder Children's Books

21st Century Debates Series

Genetics • Surveillance • Internet • Media • Artificial Intelligence • Climate Change • Energy • Rainforests • Waste, Recycling and Reuse • Endangered Species • Air Pollution • An Overcrowded World? • Food Supply • Water Supply • Transport • Global Debt • The Drugs Trade• Terrorism

Produced for Hodder Wayland by White-Thomson Publishing Ltd, 2/3 St Andrew's Place, Lewes, East Sussex BN7 1UP

© 2002 White-Thomson Publishing Ltd

Project editor: Kelly Davis
Commissioning editor: Steve White-Thomson
Proofreader: David C. Sills, Proof Positive Reading Service
Series and book design: Chris Halls, Mind's Eye Design
Picture research: Shelley Noronha, Glass Onion Pictures

British Library Cataloguing in Publication Data
Foley, Ronan
  World Health. - (21st Century Debates)
  1. World Health - Juvenile literature
  I. Title. II. Davis, Kelly
  362.1

ISBN 0 7502 3950 6

Printed in Hong Kong by Wing King Tong Co. Ltd

Hodder Children's Books, a division of Hodder Headline Ltd, 338 Euston Road, London NW1 3BH

Picture acknowledgements: EASI-ER 10 (Rob Bowden); Ecoscene 57 (Alan Towse); Eye Ubiquitous 35 (Leon Schadeberg); HWPL 11, 17 (Rolando Pujol), 38 (Gordon Clements), 51; Impact 34 (John Cole), 52 (Jeremy Nicholl), 58 (Mark Henley), cover foreground (Caroline Penn); Panos Pictures 6 (Peter Barker), 7 (J. Holmes), 8 (Giacomo Pirozzi), 16 (Barbara Klass), 18 (Betty Press), 30 (Sean Sprague), 39 (Trygve Bolstad), 42 (Clive Shirley), 48 (Chris Stowers), 50 (Chris Sattleberger), 53 (John Miles); Popperfoto 4 (Daniel LeClair), 5 and 43 (Kamal Kishore), 12 (Jean-Paul Pelissier), 24 (Mike Nelson), 41 (Dylan Martinez), 44 (Chris Wlikins), 45 (Pawel Kopczynski), 46 (Rafiqur Rahman), 55, 56; Science Photo Library 19 (Dr Linda Stannard), 20 (St Bartholomew's Hospital), 21 (National Library of Medicine), 33 (Gounot Bsip), 37 (Robert Isear), cover background (Tek Image); Topham 14 (David Giles), 22, 25 (Tony Harris); WHO/UNAIDS 28; WTPix 26, 49.

Cover: foreground picture shows immunization in a rural health clinic, Andhra Pradesh, India; background picture shows an overhead view of medical equipment, lit from behind.

CONTENTS

A HEALTHY WORLD?

What is health?

The definition of health used by the World Health Organization (WHO) is 'a state of complete physical, mental and social well-being and not merely the absence of disease or infirmity'. This means that a person's health includes their mental condition and their social position as well as the condition of their body. However, this describes a very high standard of health, and it is clear that a great many people in the world do not have a healthy life according to this definition.

A Honduran farmer looks at his drought-stricken corn in the year 2000. Lack of food is a major cause of ill-health in many parts of the world.

Patterns of health and disease

To get a clearer picture of world health, we need to look at global patterns of health and disease. This can be achieved in a number of ways. First, we need to find out about the present state of the world's health. We can do this by measuring various indicators, such as life expectancy at birth and infant mortality (the number of babies who die before their first birthday). Then, having examined these statistics in more detail, we can attempt to understand and explain them. We also need to explore the causes of disease and ill-health. Some of these causes are biological and environmental and others are linked more closely with politics, society, culture and economics.

Why do some people live longer?

The patterns and causes of illness and disease across the globe are too numerous to describe individually. This book will look at some of the indicators used to measure world health and will focus on selected diseases, in order to understand specific patterns in particular countries and continents. For instance, why is it that a child born in 2001 in Uganda can expect to live to the age of forty-three, whereas a child born in the same year in Australia can expect to live to eighty? This is just one example of the huge differences, or inequalities, in health that exist around the world. Many factors, including environment, living conditions, access to clean water, good medicines, cheap healthcare and healthy food, play a part in explaining these different health patterns.

Indian villagers collect drinking water from an almost dried-up well. A clean, safe water supply is crucial to health.

VIEWPOINT

'Poverty is the main source of ill health.'
Dr Gro Harlem Brundtland, Director-General of the WHO, commenting on the fact that a fifth of the world's population live in absolute poverty

FACT

The chance of a child dying before his or her fifth birthday varies greatly around the world. The numbers range from 5 per 1,000 live births in Sweden to 331 per 1,000 live births in Niger. This means that over 30 per cent of children die before their fifth birthday in Niger.

FACT

The proportion of aid to developing countries that is spent on health and population policies varies, on average, between 3 per cent and 20 per cent. In 1996, total aid spent on the health and population sector was over US$3 billion but aid levels have since decreased.

An unequally healthy world?

The World Health Organization (WHO) tries to improve health across the world. To achieve this, they need to know more about the kinds of inequalities that exist. For example, why do the same diseases kill more people in some places than others? Is it mainly to do with their physical environment, genetic inheritance, economic and political systems, or access to good-quality healthcare? Or are there other factors, such as diet, lifestyle and culture, that are also significant?

People living in a slum in Nairobi, Kenya. Children who grow up in slums often suffer poor health due to lack of hygiene.

Many countries, especially those in the developing world, lack either the money or the resources to look after public health properly. They do the best they can with what little they have. People in the same country may also live very different lives in very different physical surroundings, ranging from wealthy suburbs to shanty towns.

VIEWPOINT

'The UK National Health Service (NHS) will provide a universal service for all based on clinical need, not ability to pay. Public funds will be devoted solely to NHS patients.'
UK NHS Core Principles

The health debate

Health is a topic of great concern to everyone, as shown by the number of stories in the media about ill-health, disease and 'health scares'. The way in which governments look after their population's health is also the subject of regular debate. In the past decade there has been a lot of discussion in the UK, the USA and Canada about whether each country's national health care system is working as well as it should. In the developing world, economic and family structures are being devastated by infectious diseases like HIV/AIDS.

The WHO's *World Health Report* for 1998 asked a number of questions about the future for world health. Will people get healthier, with new medical advances helping us to live longer? Or will new diseases and failing drugs cancel out these gains? Will we conquer malnutrition, obesity, drug abuse, poverty, depression and the common cold? Will deaths from heart disease and cancer finally begin to decline? Will the gap between the health of rich and poor in the world grow ever wider? Questions such as these can help us understand the current state of the world's health and predict its future.

VIEWPOINT

'In countries where there has never been an effective free public healthcare system, people are used to buying drugs and treatment from unregulated private doctors and chemists. The difference today is that more public healthcare systems are introducing formal charges.'

Panos Briefing (the PANOS Institute is a worldwide non-governmental organization providing independent information on health and other matters)

Food aid being unloaded in Cambodia – a short-term answer to the world's vast health imbalances.

The cost of staying alive

In the developing world, over two million children die each year from different forms of preventable infections such as measles and whooping cough that they could have been vaccinated against. In the case of diarrhoeal diseases like dysentery, many of these deaths could be prevented by simple medicines such as re-hydration solutions (which mix salts and sugar with clean water to re-hydrate the body). At the same time, it costs several hundred dollars, on average, to accommodate one patient for one day in a normal US hospital. This would be enough money to buy daily re-hydration solutions for several hundred children in Africa.

A nurse in Angola shows a young mother how to mix oral re-hydration solution.

Diseases of age

In the developed world, although people are living longer, there has been a big increase in cancers, heart and circulatory problems, and other diseases of old age. These are now the main causes of death, as development and better access to healthcare have lessened the grip of infectious diseases in these parts of the world.

Yet the majority of the world's people, roughly 80 per cent, live in the developing world. People are living longer there too, so the numbers suffering specific diseases of old age are also greater. For example, heart disease caused 3 million deaths in the developed world in 1998. But in the same year it caused the death of 10 million people in the developing world. This gives some indication of the global scale of these health problems.

The newest threat

Some of the most urgent problems in world health concern the HIV/AIDS virus which affects both the developed and developing world. Again, the scale of the problem is far greater in the developing world. The search for a cure for HIV/AIDS continues urgently. This is a process that is linked to politics and economics, as it is partly driven by individual countries' governments, partly by the WHO and partly by pharmaceutical companies who make the drugs used to treat those suffering from HIV/AIDS.

At the same time the importance of preventive medicine and health education should not be underestimated. WHO initiatives, such as vaccinations, disease eradication programmes and specific campaigns to educate people about disease prevention, have been and continue to be a major factor in the fight to improve the world's health.

FACT

In 2000, three communicable diseases killed 5.4 million people. Malaria killed 1 million, tuberculosis killed 1.9 million, and HIV/AIDS killed almost 2.5 million. Most of these deaths occurred in the developing world.

DEBATE

When science and medicine deliver new drugs, therapies and methods to improve health, who is able to afford them? What should be done to help those who cannot afford them?

MEASURING HEALTH

POLIO ERADICATION CAMPAIGN IN
KENYA 1999

KICK POLIO OUT OF KENYA NOW!

Take your child under 5 years for Polio
Immunization on
23rd or 24th October 1999
and again on
27th or 28th November 1999
At your nearest immunization post.
KICK POLIO! KICK POLIO! OUT OF KENYA

DFID DANIDA

A Polio Eradication Campaign
poster, promoting immunization
in Kenya in 1999.

Key indicators

Many countries do not hold detailed
information on all aspects of health and
disease. Experts comparing health in the developed
and developing world therefore concentrate on key
indicators, such as life expectancy (the number of
years a person or group can expect to live),
morbidity rates (the number of people with an
illness or poor health in relation to the total
population), and mortality rates (deaths per 1,000
people) for a variety of illnesses. Other important
yardsticks include levels of available healthcare,
such as numbers of hospitals, doctors, nurses and
other medical staff, and per capita (or per person)
spending on health.

Tip of the iceberg
One difficulty with measuring diseases and
disabilities is that some of them are hard to define
and even harder to measure. This does not mean
that certain diseases and disabilities, such as mental
illness, are not important. It is just that it is easier
to gather information on sicknesses which cause
obvious physical symptoms. Measures that are
commonly used include disease incidence (the
number of new cases of a disease found in a given
area in a given time period) and the severity of the
disease (how badly it affects individual sufferers).

Again it is difficult, for example, to measure the
incidence and severity of cases of a disease like
African trypanosomiasis (sleeping sickness) in sub-
Saharan Africa. Almost 45,000 cases were reported
in 1999 but the WHO estimates that the number

of people affected is ten times greater, because many people carry the parasite without showing symptoms.

An integrated solution?

As the WHO and, indeed, many national governments have a limited amount of money to spend on improving world health, it is important to spend the available funds effectively. In 1993 the World Bank's World Development Report identified a joint initiative by the WHO and the United Nations Children's Fund (UNICEF), called Integrated Management of Childhood Illness (IMCI), as the intervention likely to have the biggest impact in reducing disease globally.

Many children in the developing world suffer from several diseases at once. By using an integrated approach, children can be treated for a number of linked health problems at the same time. For example, if a child is being treated for malaria, the child's mother can also be given information about the benefits of immunization, about improving her family's diet and about using bed-nets to protect against malaria-carrying mosquitoes.

FACT

In Tanzania, in districts where IMCI is in place, health worker performance has improved and parents/guardians are happier with the care their children receive. In rural Kenya, IMCI led to savings of at least 50 per cent in the cost of drugs per child treated in 1999.

An immunization clinic in Karachi, Pakistan. Mass immunization campaigns have been a very effective weapon in the fight against disease.

Jeanne Calment, from France, who died in August 1997 at the age of 122, the world's oldest woman.

Living longer and healthier lives

At the end of the Second World War, people all over the world lived on average to their mid-forties. By the 1990s, they could expect to live to their mid-sixties. The main reasons for global increase in lifespan since 1950 include reduced child mortality, better housing, water supply and sanitation (washing and toilet facilities), improved healthcare and advances in medicines such as antibiotics and vaccination.

Unfortunately, AIDS has had a big impact on these rates in certain parts of the developing world. For instance, as a result of AIDS the average life expectancy in some African countries, like Zimbabwe and Mozambique, has decreased significantly. Despite this, it remains true that people are generally living longer.

VIEWPOINT

'Over the next quarter-century, Europe is projected to retain its title of "oldest" region in the world. Currently, elderly people represent around 20 per cent of the total population and will represent 25 per cent by 2020'
WHO Factsheet No. 135. 1998

Life expectancy at birth for men and women born in 2000		
Country	Men	Women
Australia	77.02	82.87
Canada	76.16	83.13
UK	75.13	80.66
US	74.37	80.05
Denmark	74.12	79.47
Cuba	74.02	78.94
China	69.81	73.59
Russia	62.12	72.83
Indonesia	65.9	70.75
Brazil	58.96	67.73
Nepal	58.65	57.77
Uganda	42.59	44.17
Zimbabwe	38.51	35.7
Mozambique	37.25	35.62

Source: CIA World Fact Book, 2001

Another striking feature of the figures for life expectancy is the difference between men and women. In the developed world, in countries like Australia, Canada and the UK, men live to their mid to late seventies, whereas women live on average about six years longer. That gap is much smaller and, in some cases, reversed in developing world countries like Nepal and Zimbabwe.

The main killers

The WHO collects data each year for the most common disease groups in the different regions of the world. The total number of deaths worldwide in 2000 was 55.7 million. South-East Asia had the highest number of deaths, 14.16 million, due to its large but poor population. Communicable (infectious) diseases are significant killers in the developing world in particular. They account for almost 70 per cent of all deaths in Africa and over 40 per cent in South-East Asia and the Eastern Mediterranean.

Although AIDS does not appear very important worldwide, when compared with the number of deaths due to heart disease, cancer or other communicable diseases, it is catching up fast. However, of all AIDS deaths in 2000 (2.94 million), over 80 per cent (2.39 million) were in Africa.

Heart disease is a major cause of death in the Americas (34.4 per cent of all deaths), Europe (51.4 per cent), South-East Asia (28.9 per cent) and the Western Pacific (31.2 per cent), compared to the rest of the world. This is partly due to stress, diet and lifestyle.

Cancers account for 12.4 per cent of all world deaths and for close to 20 per cent of all deaths in Europe and the Americas. Collecting this data each year enables the WHO and national health organizations to trace patterns of mortality over time.

Dying young

A final key measure of world health is the infant mortality rate (IMR). The infant mortality rate is the number of children per 1,000 births who die in the first year of life. This has been steadily decreasing in developing countries because of improved sanitation, reduced levels of infectious disease (partly due to vaccination) and better health education. In the Central African Republic, for example, the rate has declined from 197 per 1,000 in the 1950s to 96 per 1,000 in the 1990s. (During the same period, the IMR for the UK has decreased from 24 to 6.) Despite rapid decline, infant mortality and mortality for

A baby being treated at a hospital in Rwanda. Even though they are sometimes poorly equipped, hospitals in the developing world are crucial to local health.

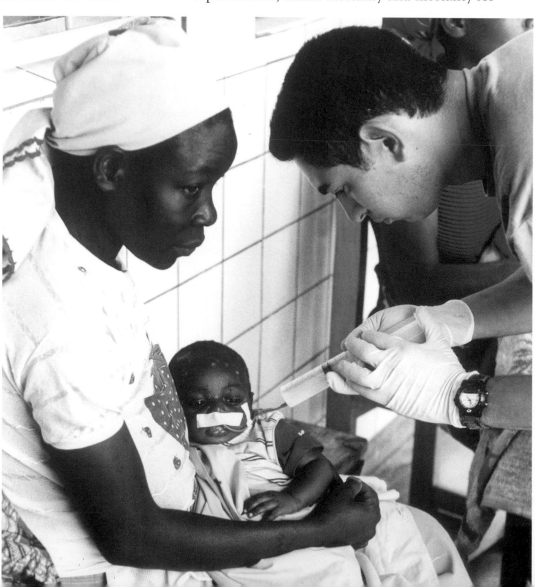

children under five remains a much greater problem in countries like the Central African Republic than in the developed world.

Measuring disease

Measuring morbidity (illness) is more difficult than measuring mortality. Defining an illness is difficult, as the seriousness and length of the illness has to be taken into account. Malaria is a good example of these difficulties. Although 1.1 million people in developing countries died of malaria in 1998, this figure is dwarfed by the number of times that people suffered from the disease seriously enough to be admitted to hospital (a clinical episode). In the same year there were between 300 and 500 million clinical episodes.

Children under five, for example, often suffer from malaria for many years and may have as many as six bouts annually. This damages the child's physical and mental development and has long-term effects on their health. By finding out which diseases are causing the greatest health problems, national and international agencies can target health education and disease prevention initiatives more effectively.

Finding out about illness

It is usually easier to measure morbidity in the developed world. There is more complete information on people's use of healthcare because most hospitals in the developed world keep records of hospital admissions. These records allow medical staff to calculate rates for specific diseases, including different forms of cancer, and respiratory and infectious diseases such as TB, HIV/AIDS, influenza and measles. The number of admissions can then be compared with the expected number of admissions for the local area to see whether the rates are above or below normal. In this way, unusual levels of specific diseases can be more easily identified.

FACT

More than half of all child deaths in developing countries are due to malnutrition and just five communicable diseases, namely pneumonia, diarrhoea, measles, malaria and HIV/AIDS.

Access to healthcare

Access to healthcare is important to everyone. But the quality of healthcare available to people around

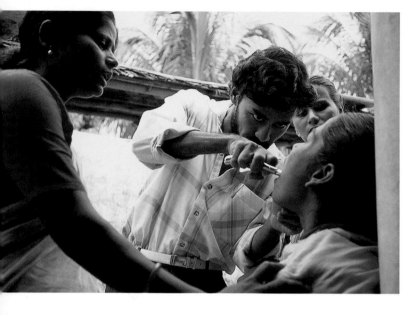

the world varies enormously, partly depending on the number of doctors per head of population. In the developing world (with the exception of countries like Costa Rica, Sri Lanka and Cuba) there are far fewer doctors, and in all countries there are more doctors in the towns and cities than in the countryside. This is partly because being a doctor is a business, and doctors always make more money working in urban areas as they have lower costs and more patients. Other services that provide valuable local health services include pharmacies and dentists.

A dentist working outdoors in Bangladesh. Dentists and pharmacies are the only source of healthcare in some areas.

Health spending

Another common measure of access to healthcare is the percentage of a country's total economic resources, or Gross Domestic Product (GDP), spent on health. Spending on health tends to be higher in countries like the US which have a mainly private healthcare system, funded by insurance payments.

However, spending a lot on healthcare does not always guarantee good health. There is no direct link, for example, between percentage of GDP spent on health and increased life expectancy. The International Monetary Fund (IMF) estimated that in 1999 Heavily Indebted Poor Countries (HIPCs) spent, on average, around 2.1 per cent of GDP on health. Yet, while 30 per cent of the better-off people in those poor countries had experienced a 'health benefit', only 13 per cent of the poorest had benefited.

Enough beds to go round?

Access to healthcare can also be measured by counting the number of spaces in clinics and hospitals relative to the population. During a health crisis, such as an epidemic, natural disaster or famine, the ability of the healthcare system to care for its population will have an impact on health. The number of hospital beds ranges from around 1.8 beds per 1,000 people in sub-Saharan Africa to around 9 per 1,000 in the developed world.

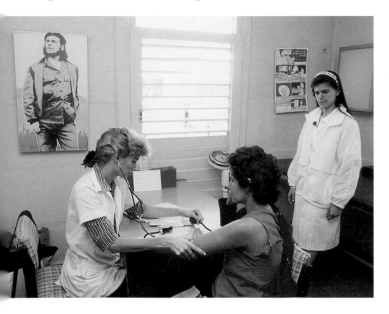

A doctor working in a Cuban medical clinic. The people of Cuba are generally very healthy, despite the country's relative poverty.

Similarly, the average number of doctors per 1,000 population ranges from 0.2 in the developing world to 2.5 in the developed world. However, it is important to realize that simply counting the numbers of doctors and hospitals is not always the best way of measuring access to health. This is especially true in developing countries where local clinics and community health workers play a vital role in improving people's health.

WORLD DISEASES

Bad bugs

Understanding how our environment can make us sick is an important first step in keeping ourselves well. Pathogens (viruses, bacteria and parasites that cause disease) exist in the natural environment and they can be transmitted from the environment to humans. For example, the tsetse fly bites humans, introducing the virus that causes sleeping sickness in Central and Southern Africa. In many diseases, such as AIDS, pathogens can be transmitted from humans to other humans. Although vaccination has removed or reduced the risk of diseases like smallpox and yellow fever, diseases such as sleeping sickness and malaria cannot be vaccinated against and remain major killers.

A child with sleeping sickness, Mali. This disease threatens 60 million people in sub-Saharan Africa.

Other pathogens can be transmitted by eating undercooked meat or by drinking water from a contaminated source. So one of the best ways to stay healthy is simply to be careful about what we eat and drink. One example of a disease which is passed on via contaminated water is schistosomiasis (or bilharzia). Each year, between 7,000 and 20,000 people die of this disease. But it has been estimated that 200 million people living in rural and semi-urban areas of the developing world were infested with the schistoma worm in 1998. This is passed on when an infected human urinates into a river or irrigation channel. The worm eggs hatch in the water and enter snails, as they need a host. The young worms then enter other humans via the contaminated water.

Migration breeds sickness

In the eighteenth and nineteenth centuries, when European nations such as Britain, Spain, Portugal and Holland were colonizing much of the world, disease moved in both directions. The colonizers and the colonized had such different immune systems that diseases could wipe out large numbers of people on first exposure. For instance, the populations of indigenous people, such as the Arawaks of the West Indies and the Aboriginals of Australia, were reduced enormously after the arrival of white settlers because they had no resistance to introduced diseases like smallpox and measles. On the other side, many colonizers also died of parasitic native diseases such as malaria, dysentery and sleeping sickness. Migration remains a major route of disease and infection to this day.

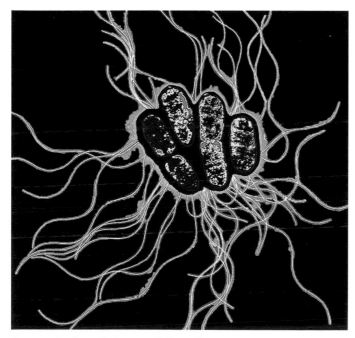

A group of salmonella bacteria. Salmonella, mainly found in undercooked poultry and eggs, can cause serious food poisoning.

A seventeenth-century doctor wearing a bird-like mask filled with sweet-smelling herbs to try to ward off the Black Death.

Plagues and epidemics

Some of the first recorded global epidemics – such as the Black Death of the Middle Ages – caused millions of deaths across whole continents. The Black Death started in China in the fourteenth century, and worked its way westwards, eventually affecting the whole of Europe and Asia. Because of their infectiousness and the lack of adequate medicines, plagues like these spread fast and killed people very quickly. The Black Death killed 10 million people in Western Europe in 1348-1349.

Between 1500 and 1900, the main killers were diseases such as dysentery, malaria and smallpox, and a great many mothers and babies also died during or just after childbirth. Rembrandt, the famous Dutch painter, had four children of whom three died within two months of birth. This was relatively common in the seventeenth century.

More dangerous than war?

More recently, the Great Influenza or 'Spanish Flu' outbreak of 1919 killed more people – 25 million worldwide – than had died in the previous four years during the First World War (around 9 million). Smallpox also used to be a big killer but gradually, during the twentieth century, world health initiatives, such as mass vaccination, weakened its grip. The last official case was cured in Somalia in 1977 and represented a huge success for the WHO vaccination programme.

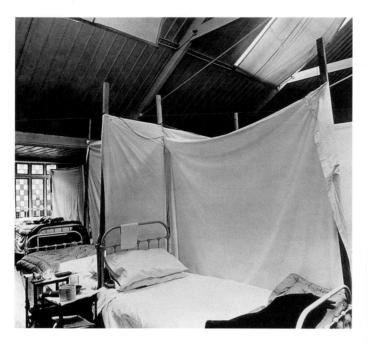

An influenza ward in an American Red Cross hospital in Paris, France, 1919.

There were also important discoveries of new drugs in the twentieth century, especially antibiotics. It is antibiotics that are perhaps our most powerful weapons against disease because they directly tackle the pathogens that cause illnesses.

Despite these successes, there are still a number of diseases, apart from HIV/AIDS and malaria, that are responsible for vast numbers of deaths in the developing world. For example, schistosomiasis (bilharzia) is found to the largest extent in Africa, and infects an estimated 200 million each year. Japanese encephalitis (brain fever) is found in South and East Asia. It is linked to irrigated rice production, and epidemic outbreaks kill a great many children. Lymphatic filariasis (elephantitis) is a mainly urban disease, though in Central Africa it is linked to irrigation. Onchocerciasis (river blindness) is found across West and Central Africa and in Central America. However, the Onchocerciasis Control Programme has eliminated the disease in large parts of West Africa.

VIEWPOINTS

'Advances in medicine have not caused the biggest decline in mortality over the previous 150 years. The real reasons have been improvements in nutrition and standards of living such as improved housing, better sanitation and healthier diets and have had very little to do with medicine'
Thomas McKeown, Professor of Social Medicine (1945 1977), University of Birmingham

'Health improvements over time still have a very strong public health background and were the work of enlightened doctors and could not have happened without them.'
Dr Simon Szreter, Social Historian, University of Cambridge

Changing causes of death

These days, infectious diseases still cause many deaths in the developing world. But in the developed world, as people have started to live longer, cancers, heart disease and strokes have now become major killers. These illnesses are not caused by poor sanitation or lack of food. More often, they are caused by other factors linked to age, lifestyle, stress and environmental conditions.

Many cancers and circulatory problems are more common in the developed world and this must be partly due to certain aspects of people's lifestyles

Doctors x-ray a patient at an American TB clinic. TB had almost been eradicated but new drug-resistant strains of the disease have developed in Eastern Europe and elsewhere.

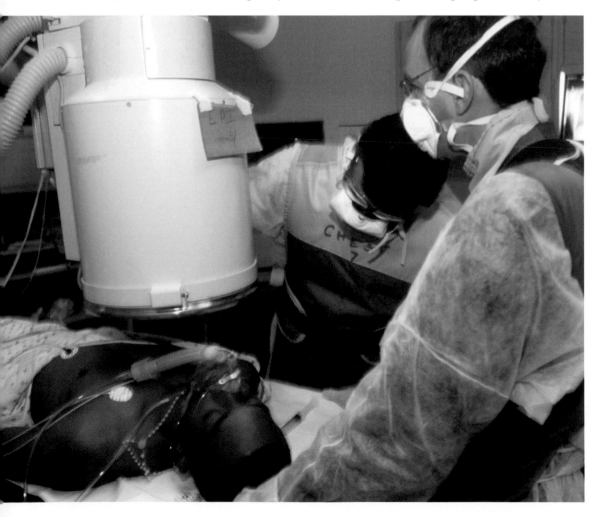

and diets. An obvious example is the link between smoking cigarettes and lung cancer, which has been widely recognized since the 1960s. Other examples include the well-established links between obesity, lack of exercise and a high-fat diet, or between liver disease and large intakes of alcohol. There are also links between health and the environment, as pollution affects our breathing and our immune systems.

Superbugs fight back

Diseases will always occur and evolve over time until researchers find cures or treatments for them. In the case of tuberculosis (TB), an infectious disease of the lungs, the disease was largely controlled in the first half of the twentieth century by improved diagnosis and the use of antibiotics and vaccines. Recently, however, TB has reappeared, especially in Eastern Europe and Russia. Even more worryingly, new strains of the virus have developed an ability to resist existing treatments. This has been caused by poor prescribing, insufficient supply of antibiotics, and patients failing to complete their course of treatment.

Diphtheria cases have also increased significantly in Russia since 1993. There were over 50,000 reported cases in 1995, whereas under the previous political system diphtheria had been effectively eliminated.

High standards of health and safety, for instance when dealing with foods and medicines, reduce the risk of disease. However, people sometimes lack the information they need in order to take simple precautions. Health education therefore plays a vital role in showing citizens of the world that behaving in a healthy way – for example, boiling water before use – will help them live longer, healthier lives.

VIEWPOINTS

'WHO and our partners will provide teams of experts to help countries use expensive but vital anti-TB drugs properly and safely, in order not to develop further drug resistance'
Dr J.W. Lee, Director, Stop-TB, WHO

'There is no country in the developing world that has a treatment compliance rate as bad as New York City. New York has 10% compliance, India has 25%, China has 80 to 90% and Mozambique managed 80% compliance during a civil war'
Christopher Murray, Harvard University, discussing the problem of getting TB patients in New York to take their medication correctly

DEBATE

The developing world is suffering a double threat to health. People are living longer and are getting diseases of old age while infectious disease rates are still very high. Which should be the priority for government spending?

Health information – a vital weapon

One of the best ways for any nation to protect the health of its citizens is to make sure they do not get ill in the first place. How can this be achieved? First, by giving people a greater awareness of their own ability to look after their own health. This requires greater spending on health promotion. However, some commentators argue that if more money is spent on health promotion less will be spent on hospitals. The optimistic view is that people will listen to the health education messages and stay healthy, and fewer hospital resources will be needed to treat them.

A Californian anti-smoking poster. In California, virtually all public places are smoke-free.

The HIV/AIDS epidemic in Africa and Asia has led to a large number of specialist health education campaigns. These explain, using easily understood language and images, how the virus is spread and how to prevent people from catching it. In the developed world there have been numerous campaigns, ranging from reducing traffic speeds in order to cut deaths on the roads to clearly explaining the health risks of tobacco products.

Living fast, dying young

Many governments use media messages (often in the form of television advertising or leaflets in doctors' surgeries) to try to persuade people to behave in a healthier way. However, the media also publicizes some famous people who appear very cool

precisely because they do 'live dangerously' –
drinking a lot of alcohol, smoking and taking drugs.
Celebrities like these may become role models for
young people, sending out an opposing media
message. These negative role models, combined
with peer pressure from friends, can often encourage
young people to make unhealthy choices.

Getting the message across

In many countries, health advertising has been
used to tackle a wide range of problems. Some of
these adverts work very powerfully; others are less
effective. For some people, an advert showing an
overdosed drug addict or the funeral of a drunk
driver's victim may have a big impact. Other
people may find it too hard-hitting, and turn away.
The best approach seems to be simply to ensure
that people are fully informed of the risks and then
let them make up their own minds.

*A British anti-drink-drive campaign
poster that uses the powerful image
of a young accident victim to convey
its message.*

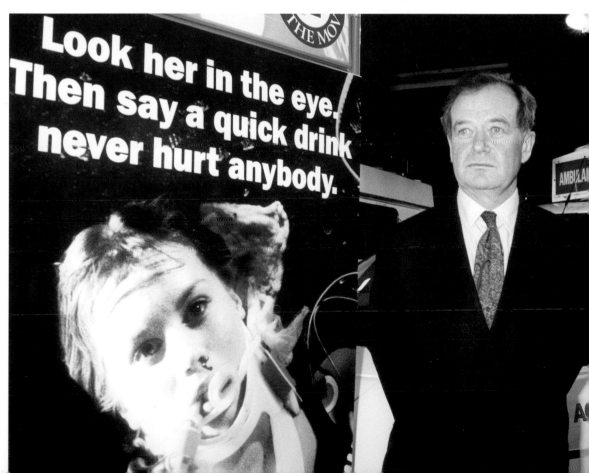

THE HIV/AIDS CRISIS

What is HIV/AIDS?

A IDS (Acquired Immune Deficiency Syndrome), and its associated virus HIV (Human Immunodeficiency Virus) is the greatest new threat to human life at the beginning of the twenty-first century. What is it? And how does it affect people?

AIDS awareness poster, Kenya. Prevention is the key to slowing the spread of AIDS.

DON'T BE FOOLED
AIDS IS NOT WITCHCRAFT
AIDS IS REAL

AVOID SEX BEFORE MARRIAGE
STICK TO ONE PARTNER
OR USE A CONDOM

Essentially, HIV attacks a person's immune system by destroying helper T-cells in the blood, removing their natural ability to cope with disease. People with HIV eventually develop full-blown AIDS. But people do not die of AIDS. People with AIDS actually die of secondary infections, such as pneumonia, respiratory failure and other diseases. These conditions are not normally fatal – they become fatal because AIDS has more or less wiped out the body's ability to cope. AIDS is normally transmitted by exchanging body fluids with a carrier of the disease, through sexual contact, by sharing needles in drug-use, or through infected blood transfusion or breast milk.

Is there a cure for the virus and how is it affecting the world's health? In the developed world, in the twenty or so years since HIV/AIDS has been recognized, many patients with the virus have been able to manage their condition through a complex cocktail of drugs. However, these drug cocktails are very expensive. For millions of HIV/AIDS sufferers in the developing world, these drugs (essential to delay the development of the full-blown virus and to prolong life) are rarely available or affordable. HIV/AIDS also has wider social and economic effects. Increased deaths of parents mean that there are huge numbers of orphaned children whose health is further affected by having to make a living in already difficult circumstances.

Recognizing the problem

People's feelings about HIV/AIDS have changed over time. Initially, in the developed world, it was most closely associated with homosexuals. It was therefore seen as a 'gay plague' and sufferers often experienced prejudice from other members of society. Later, links with other high-risk groups, such as intravenous drug-users and haemophiliacs, were identified. Yet it was not until people realized the enormous impact the disease was having on the heterosexual population and the developing world that serious attempts were made to address HIV/AIDS as the greatest threat to world health today. Now there is a special branch of the United Nations, UNAIDS, taking direct action, together with other health organizations to monitor, manage and combat the problem.

From the Golden Gate to Ghana

HIV/AIDS was first identified in San Francisco in 1981 when doctors began to notice fatal cases of pneumonia and incidences of a very rare cancer, Kaposi's Sarcoma, among the gay population. Since then, it has spread very quickly; at the end of 2001, there were 40 million cases worldwide. The disease

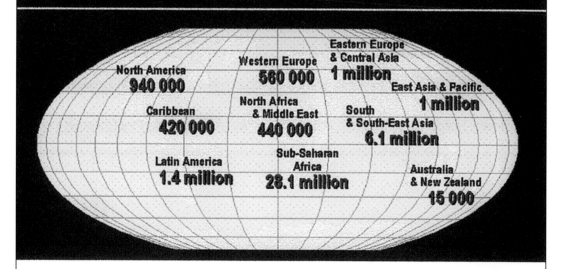

Adults and children estimated to be living with HIV/AIDS as of end 2001

North America 940 000

Western Europe 560 000

Eastern Europe & Central Asia 1 million

East Asia & Pacific 1 million

Caribbean 420 000

North Africa & Middle East 440 000

South & South-East Asia 6.1 million

Latin America 1.4 million

Sub-Saharan Africa 28.1 million

Australia & New Zealand 15 000

Total: 40 million

UNAIDS
UNICEF · UNDP · UNFPA · UNDCP
ILO · UNESCO · WHO · WORLD BANK

00002-E-4 – 1 December 2001

World Health
Organization

is particularly severe in Africa and increasingly in Asia, where it has infected the populations on a terrifying scale. Between 1981 and 2001, HIV infected about 58 million people worldwide; about 21 million people died from AIDS, 3 million in 2000 alone. AIDS is already the fourth-leading cause of death among adults and the leading cause of death in sub-Saharan Africa.

A growing problem

One of the difficulties with HIV/AIDS is knowing the scale of the epidemic. The period between infection and the onset of illness is a long one, sometimes up to eight years. Planning a strategy to combat the disease is also difficult. Until 1990, two-thirds of all cases were in the USA. But, by 1999, over 90 per cent of people living with HIV/AIDS were in the developing world. One of the areas where HIV/AIDS infection is growing fastest is in South-East Asia, in countries like Thailand and Cambodia. Promoting awareness of AIDS and educating local people on simple ways to avoid getting infected are the major priorities for a number of non-governmental organizations (NGOs) working in these countries.

Not only does the epidemic pose a huge ongoing threat to world health, it also has a long-term effect on society and development. Economically, AIDS is undoing a lot of the good work of previous decades in parts of Africa, Asia and South America. When the prevalence (or rate in the population as a whole) reaches 8 per cent, which it does in twenty African countries, economic growth is reduced by 0.8 per cent each year. The financial cost of HIV/AIDS is also enormous. In the poorest countries, care and treatment for a person with AIDS, even without intensive drug treatment, can cost as much as two or three times the individual per capita gross domestic product (GDP).

FACT

According to UNAIDS/WHO estimates, eleven men, women and children around the world contracted HIV every minute during 1998 – close to six million people in all. About 10 per cent of those infected were children. They are thought to have received the infection from their mothers, before or during birth or through breast-feeding.

The search for a cure

The major pharmaceutical companies are continuing to spend a vast amount of money in the search for a cure for HIV/AIDS. Much information has already been obtained about the virus – how it infects people and how the disease can be managed. Researchers have found a number of drug combinations which are relatively successful in isolating the virus and preventing its spread. By taking a cocktail of these drugs, a process known as Highly Active Anti-Retroviral Therapy (HAART), the life of people living with HIV/AIDS can be prolonged.

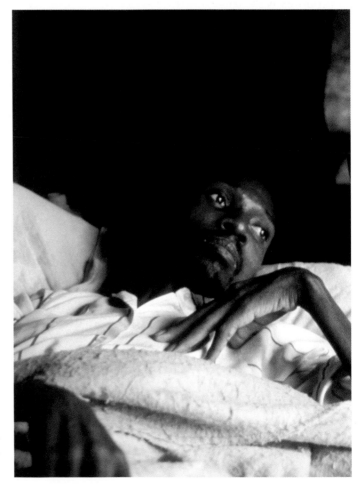

An AIDS patient in Uganda, a country that has been affected by the epidemic since the late 1970s.

However, this is a very expensive treatment and the annual cost can be as much as $10,000 per patient. As pharmaceutical companies are profit-based businesses, they make anti-HIV drugs available under patent in the developing world. Yet some countries, such as India, can produce cheaper generic (copy) versions of the drugs, which are more affordable for a population living on an average monthly salary of around $110. This debate is continuing. Recently pharmaceutical companies took the South African government to court for allowing the manufacture and distribution of cheap copies of patented drugs, but the companies were forced to withdraw their case. This was partly due to pressure from international bodies like the EU and World Trade Organization (WTO). Some pharmaceutical companies are now making deals which allow manufacturers in the developing world to make cheaper copies of drugs.

Prevention is part of the cure

Many agencies, including the WHO and UNAIDS, believe that prevention is vital in combating HIV/AIDS. Early action has had an impact in a number of countries in stopping the spread of the disease. These preventive measures include educating people about safe sex (using condoms to protect against infection), making HIV/AIDS testing, diagnosis and treatment easier, ensuring a safe blood transfusion supply, and preventing parent to child transmission of the virus. The challenge is to make these interventions across whole countries and regions and to sustain them over time. Cost-effective measures, such as public information programmes, preventive equipment and treatment of associated infections, can cost as little as $8 per case, compared to the hundreds of dollars it costs to treat each case of AIDS.

FACT

The South African government had refused to make AZT (an anti-AIDS drug) available in public clinics, saying that it was toxic even though studies had shown it could protect the unborn babies of HIV-infected mothers. This position was finally changed in late 2001.

DEBATE

To tackle the global HIV/AIDS problem, countries need to combine health education programmes with cost-effective treatment. Which do you think should take priority?

HEALTH INEQUALITIES AROUND THE WORLD

What causes health inequalities?

Around the world, people are treated for ill-health in a wide variety of places, ranging from their homes to the intensive care units of hospitals. In the developing world, patients may turn to local healers and poorly staffed and equipped clinics. Sadly, it is often those areas which have the most need for healthcare who receive the least.

On a global level, there is a stark contrast in people's health in the developed and the developing world. Within particular regions, there are also variations between rural and urban areas, and between different groups within societies. Minority groups, such as gypsies in Western Europe and refugees in many parts of the world, experience greater health problems than 'settled' populations.

The healthcare business
In the developed world, healthcare has become a large and complex business. Western medicine tends to view the human body as a 'machine' and places a strong emphasis on the use of medical interventions to 'fix' it when it stops functioning.

FACT

There are 20-25 million refugees and displaced people throughout the world. Because they have no permanent homes, they face particular difficulty in gaining access to medical treatment, food and water.

Primary healthcare in the local community is mainly provided by doctors or general practitioners (GPs). Local clinics provide treatment where possible, followed up by referral to hospitals and specialists for severe cases.

In the developing world, generally speaking, there is a less structured system. There are fewer hospitals and they are more spread out (mainly in the larger towns and cities). Much healthcare is therefore provided by local clinics. In general, there is far less access to healthcare than in the developed world.

Different approaches to the body

Whereas western medicine treats the body as a machine which can be fixed and repaired, other societies have very different beliefs about human health. For example, Chinese medicine is based on the concept of a person's essential spirit or *chi*, which needs to be correctly balanced. Herbal medicines or treatments such as acupuncture (which requires needles to be inserted at certain points on the body) may be used to restore the balance of the *chi*. These systems are ancient types of medicine, sometimes referred to as 'alternative' medicine (as opposed to conventional, western medicine).

An Ayurvedic practitioner checks a patient's pulse. Ayurveda is traditional Indian medicine based on the prevention of disease through diet, exercise and herbalism. It is one of several alternatives to conventional medicine in the West.

Different ways of organizing healthcare

Around the world, healthcare is arranged and funded in different ways. In some countries, like the UK, doctors and hospital services, funded by public taxation, are free for everyone. In other countries, like the US, the more you can afford to pay, the better the healthcare you can buy. Expensive private hospitals and specialist doctors are paid for by medical insurance. There are also many countries, like France and Brazil, that combine private and public medicine.

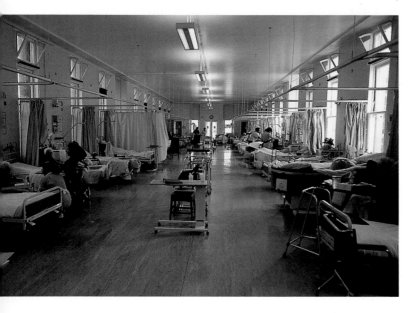

A well-equipped modern ward in a London hospital.

Whatever the system, people may experience wide variations in affordability, waiting times and service quality. One of the biggest challenges facing the WHO and other national and international health organizations is how to close this gap between public and private, and make better services available to all.

Who foots the bill?

In many countries, public spending on health has been reduced dramatically and governments have had to find new ways of funding public healthcare. One approach is to introduce user fees (where the patient pays for the service) but these are problematic for poorer people. For instance, when fees were introduced into West African countries like Nigeria and Ghana, the use of hospitals and clinics declined by 50 per cent within a few weeks. The people could not afford the medical treatment they needed.

Insurance schemes are another way of funding healthcare. Under such systems, people can spread the cost of healthcare over time. In many countries employers pay into the scheme as well. However, there are problems with insurance schemes in countries like Bangladesh and Vietnam which have little formal employment and large poor, rural populations.

Private versus public

In the developed world, healthcare is funded in several different ways. In the US, private health insurance schemes are used by up to 80 per cent of the population. For those people who cannot afford adequate health insurance, such as the very poor and the old, there are government-funded schemes known as Medicaid and Medicare. For those who can afford it, the US provides probably the best healthcare in the world. In other parts of the world, however, moves towards privately funded healthcare have arguably resulted in increased inequalities.

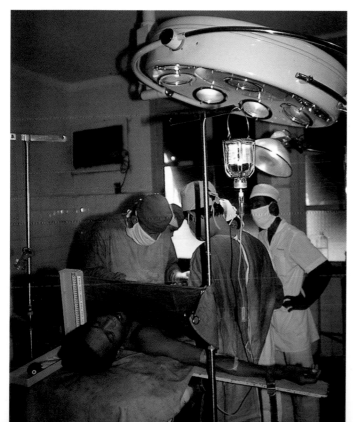

This hospital in Cambodia has only the most basic equipment, with no electronic monitors to check the patient's breathing and heart rate during surgery.

DEBATE

It is a good idea for wealthier people to pay for private medicine because it means that fewer people will be making demands on the public health service. Do you agree?

The global drugs market

Medical drugs are big business. It is estimated that the global pharmaceutical market will be worth $400 billion per year by 2002. As with any business, pharmaceutical companies rely on expanding their trade and spend a lot of money on marketing their products worldwide. The most common pain relief pill, Aspirin, now available all over the world, was developed by a German company as early as the 1890s.

Some would argue that the largest multinational drug companies now have too much power over the price and development of medicines. However, it can take over ten years to develop and market a successful new product (at an average cost of £350 million/$500 million). Companies need to see a return on their investment.

Conflicts of interest

There is, according to the WHO, 'a conflict of interest between the legitimate business goals of drugs manufacturers and the social, medical and economic needs of providers and the public to select and use drugs in the most rational way'. The WHO has attempted to tackle the problem of aggressive marketing of drugs by introducing an ethical policy for drug promotion. Some observers feel that these guidelines have been generally ignored.

There is another conflict of interest regarding new drugs. Pharmaceutical companies are thought to prefer investing in research on drugs for use in the developed world rather than those needed in the developing world. As so many patients in Africa and Asia would be unable to pay for them, the argument goes, it does not make business sense to invest in them.

The benefits of drugs

It would be wrong to underestimate the benefits that certain drugs, such as antibiotics, can offer. Over time, initially expensive drugs become cheaper and more affordable in the developing world where they are most needed. There are also a number of international corporations and foundations providing free drugs to help combat disease. For example, one American foundation provides free supplies of ivermectin, which helps prevent onchocerciasis (river blindness). Meanwhile, a Japanese company has helped the WHO to supply drugs for TB prevention in sufficient quantities to treat about 800,000 patients per year in some thirty-five countries.

Drug capsules being checked before packaging. The multi-billion-dollar pharmaceutical industry has made a significant contribution to improvements in world health over the past 100 years.

DEBATE

When patients cannot afford the life-saving drugs they need, but drug companies cannot cut their prices without reducing the money available for new medical research, who should foot the bill?

WHO cares

The WHO was set up by the United Nations after the Second World War to try to reduce health inequalities across the world. The WHO had a budget of about $1.8 billion in 1998-9. Some of the WHO's strategies include large-scale vaccination programmes and other preventive methods, as well as important public health education campaigns. The WHO also emphasizes the link between poverty and health, and the advantages of putting money into health – for both the developed and the developing world.

A number of other agencies are fighting to reduce inequalities in world health. For example, the World Bank has been providing support in the areas of health, nutrition and population since the 1970s. It now offers advice and loans to more than ninety countries in the developing world. The World Bank also co-operates closely with non-governmental organizations (NGOs) as well as the governments of individual countries.

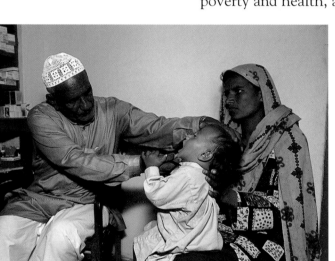

Local clinics, like this one in Pakistan, play a vital role in international public health programmes.

UNICEF spends about a third of its expenditure on child health but also funds development in the areas of water supply and sanitation that have a direct effect on world health. There are a large number of NGOs (such as the International Red Cross and Red Crescent Societies, Oxfam, Medicins Sans Frontières and Concern) who all include health as a part of their role. Some projects deal with emergency medical support, while others have long-term health as a specific objective.

A child with a Red Cross worker at a refugee camp, Sierra Leone.

Starting from scratch

A key policy aimed at reducing health inequalities is Primary Healthcare (PHC), developed in 1978 and supported by all agencies. The PHC approach has helped reduce infant mortality worldwide from 90 per 1,000 live births in 1975 to 59 per 1,000 in 1995, while immunization coverage increased from 20 per cent to 80 per cent between 1980 and 1990. The proportion of people in developing countries who have access to safe drinking water has increased from 38 per cent in the 1970s to 66 per cent in 1990, and adequate sanitation rates have increased from 32 per cent to 53 per cent. Yet, despite these improvements, together with economic changes and a greater move towards private health systems, inequalities in public health provision still remain a major issue in world health.

VIEWPOINT

'There is solid evidence to prove that investing wisely in health will help the world take a giant leap out of poverty. We can drastically reduce the global burden of disease. If we manage, hundreds of millions of people will be better able to fulfil their potential, enjoy their legitimate human rights and be driving forces in development.'
Dr Gro Harlem Brundtland, Director-General of the WHO

HEALTH AND THE ENVIRONMENT

The air we breathe

Our environment makes a big difference to our health. For example, in London in the 1950s, the thick chemical fog known as smog, caused by the use of coal for heating, was the direct reason for large numbers of people dying prematurely each year from bronchial infections.

Nowadays, cities like Jakarta in Indonesia and Mexico City suffer air pollution caused by traffic fumes, the use of polluting technology, and high levels of sunlight which encourage reactions between the different pollutants. The main impact is on people who suffer from respiratory disease.

Clean pipes, healthy lives

The quality of our water also affects our health. For example, in US cities such as Baltimore and New York, a link has been discovered between lead piping in older housing and children's health. The water running through the pipes gets contaminated over time, damaging the health of children who drink it.

In the developing world, access to clean water is even more important, as many of the major infectious diseases are water-borne. Cholera is caused by eating food or drinking water containing *Vibrio cholerae*. Symptoms include diarrhoea and vomiting. If left untreated, death can occur rapidly – sometimes within hours. Cholera can spread very quickly when people are living in overcrowded conditions, with unprotected water sources and no safe disposal of human waste. These conditions are found in poor countries and in many refugee camps.

> **FACT**
>
> In 1994 in a refugee camp in Goma, Democratic Republic of the Congo, a major cholera epidemic took place. There were an estimated 58,000-80,000 cases and 23,800 people died within a month.

A couple cycle across a bridge over a polluted river on the outskirts of Hanoi. Vietnam's industry, much of it antiquated, is pouring pollutants into the environment.

Dangerous chemicals

Pesticides (chemicals that destroy insects and other pests) and fertilizers (containing nitrates) are used on farms all over the world. Many of these chemicals leave traces in our food. As another consequence, high levels of nitrates may end up in drinking water, leading to severe illness or even death for some bottle-fed infants.

Other toxins can also have serious effects. For instance, in the 1950s, residents of the area around Minimata Bay, Japan, suddenly fell victim to a mysterious illness that ultimately caused 1,004 deaths. Eventually it was found that the outbreak had been caused by a spill of mercury into the sea. The mercury was absorbed by shellfish that were in turn eaten by the local people. It took over six years to identify and explain the problem.

VIEWPOINTS

'The World Health Organization estimates that every year 3 million people suffer acute, severe pesticide poisoning. Over 20,000 may die. One tablespoon of spilled pesticide concentrate could pollute the water supply of 200,000 people for a day.'
Pesticide Action Network UK (Part of PAN International) website

'Pesticide use within modern agricultural practices can play an important role in protecting crops and in ensuring high quality food products. Regardless of farming practice, some residue may reach groundwater. Data from the UK shows that where excesses do occur the pesticides concerned are detected in only very small quantities'
UK Environment Agency

FACT

It is now widely accepted that the Chernobyl nuclear disaster has led to a massive increase in thyroid (throat) cancers in the three countries most affected, Belarus, Russia and Ukraine. Belarus has shown a hundred-fold increase, from 0.3 per million in 1981-85 to 30.6 per million in 1991-94.

Disastrous accidents

From time to time, accidents occur which have a massive impact on the local environment and human health. Perhaps the best-known example was the accident at the Chernobyl Nuclear Power Station in the Ukraine in 1986, when a cloud of radioactive material was blown into the air and carried across most of Europe. It is estimated that at least 10,000 people have since died of various cancers due to the accident. The impact was most severe in the area immediately around the plant and in the surrounding countryside of Northern Ukraine and across the border in Belarus. But the effects were also felt further away, in Scandinavia, where cancer rates in animals and humans increased sharply in the months and even years following the accident.

In India in 1984, the Union Carbide factory at Bhopal accidentally released a cloud of poisonous gas. The official death toll is now more than 5,000, but activists say the real number of deaths from

Contaminated area outside the Chernobyl nuclear reactor, Ukraine. The fallout from the accident affected health all over Europe.

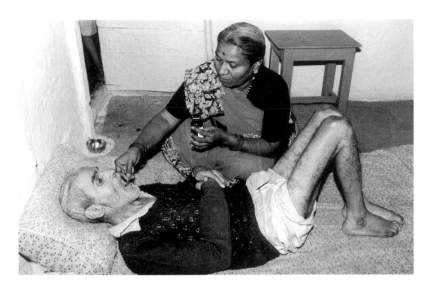

A Bhopal victim being given medicine by his wife.

gas-related illnesses is closer to 20,000. No one has yet decided who will clean up the toxic waste which environmental groups say is still seeping into drinking water from the ruins of the plant. The impact of such accidents on the people who live in the surrounding area will vary according to the specific situation but many could be prevented if health and safety laws were followed.

Maps can save lives
Large-scale outbreaks of diseases, such as AIDS or cholera, are known as epidemics, and the study of these outbreaks is called epidemiology. Experts study what causes the disease, where it starts, and how it progresses, and this knowledge can help them to predict where the disease will occur next. Sometimes mapping the disease in this way helps to explain its cause. For example, in London in the 1850s, Dr John Snow mapped where cholera deaths had happened and found that they were mostly close to a water pump in Broad Street that the victims had used. He suggested to the authorities that they close the pump and test the water. When they did, they found that the water was contaminated, and the deaths stopped straight away.

FACT

Apart from the immediate death toll caused by volcanic eruptions, floods and earthquakes, enormous health problems result from the homelessness and destruction of sewers that follow. Other examples have included earthquakes in Turkey (1999, Izmit, 17,000 dead) and India (2001, Gujarat, 30,000 dead).

Living on the edge

People on very low incomes may know that they are living in high-risk areas but be unable to afford to move away or may choose to stay. For instance, people in Bangladesh know that floods are relatively common in low-lying parts of the country, and thousands have drowned there over the past few decades. This risk is likely to increase with global warming as 90 per cent of Bangladesh is less than 10 metres above current sea level. However, most Bangladeshis have no choice but to stay.

An American boy walks through the rubble of his home in Granada Hills, California which was destroyed in an earthquake in 1994.

FACT

The largest recorded earthquake in recent times occurred in 1556 in Senshi Province, China. It is estimated to have killed 830,000 people. More recently, hurricanes and floods caused the deaths of between 500,000 and 1 million people in Bangladesh in 1970.

Meanwhile, in the developed world, many residents of California live in a high-risk earthquake zone, knowing that the forecasts suggest a very large earthquake will happen along the San Andreas Fault within the next few decades. Although awareness of the danger is strong in both places, people still risk their health by living there.

Our homes, our health

People's health also largely depends on their home environment. Poor-quality housing, cold, damp and built with unsafe materials, can give rise to numerous illnesses. Statistics from many countries show that people who live in large houses with

good facilities have better general health than people who live in run-down apartment blocks and shanty towns. For example, studies in South Africa in the 1980s showed that black people had much higher rates of tuberculosis (TB) infection, caused by poor housing, overcrowding, poor nutrition and inadequate sanitation in the townships in which they were forced to live.

Debris lies scattered near Bhuj, in India, after a massive earthquake in 2001 in which thousands died.

Regulating public health and safety

The United Nations recognizes that everyone is entitled to live and work in a safe environment. Although people in poorer countries or in cities may not always have a choice about where they live and work, most governments, especially those in the developed world, have laws governing health and safety in the home and workplace. Since these laws were passed, there have been far fewer deaths in industrial accidents in the developed world. But there is still much to be done to make life safer. Accidents like the one which occurred in Israel in May 2001, when a hotel floor collapsed during a wedding party, killing twenty-three people, still happen surprisingly often.

VIEWPOINT

'Occupational working conditions take a heavy toll in many developing countries: bad working conditions or exposure to toxic chemicals, dust and allergenic or carcinogenic agents affect millions, as does exposure to insecticides and other toxic chemicals on the land. WHO estimates that there are 217 million cases of occupational diseases and 250 million cases of injury at work every year.'
WHO, World Health Report, 1998

National governments and international
organizations aim to lessen the effect of the
environment on public health. The most obvious
way of doing this is by responding very quickly to
accidents and emergencies. Floods, earthquakes
and industrial accidents can have very serious
impacts on water supply, air quality and emergency
food provision.

*Flood victims in Bangladesh.
Pressure on land means that many
Bangladeshis have no choice but to
live in low-lying flood zones.*

A sustainable environment for health

Apart from the immediate aftermath of an accident
or environmental catastrophe, longer-term
planning is needed. Environmental factors that
have to be managed to safeguard public health
include, for example, protection of the water
supply. During periods of drought, over-extraction
of groundwater in coastal areas can cause a fall in

the water table (the level of water stored underground). Salt water from the sea may then seep through the ground, introducing salt and other impurities into the system and forcing people to use unsafe drinking water. If such effects cannot be prevented, alternative water supplies should be installed to counter the health risks involved.

Farming methods also have major effects on public health. For instance, some of the pesticides used on crops contain chemicals that are harmful to humans when consumed in large quantities over a long period. Pesticides can also make health problems worse through their impact on the environment, for instance by killing birds and other creatures that normally control the populations of disease-spreading insects such as tsetse flies and mosquitoes.

Life chances

In public health terms, a person's 'life chance' means their chance of living to the average age in their society. There are risks associated with addiction to drugs, alcohol, cigarettes and other substances. There is also evidence that homeless people and people who live in hostels and shelters have a much lower 'life chance' than those who have their own accommodation.

In the developed world, statistics from British cities such as London and Brighton show that homeless men aged sixteen to twenty-nine are up to forty times more likely to die prematurely than men living in normal circumstances. In the developing world, the situation is even worse for groups such as pavement dwellers in India and street children in Brazil. There are around 10 million children living on the streets in Brazilian cities, many of whom live short, violent lives. Their health is affected by poverty, solvent and drug abuse, and lack of proper nutrition and sanitation.

FOOD, POVERTY, DEVELOPMENT AND HEALTH

Rich, fatty diets are a major cause of ill-health in the modern world.

You are what you eat

Nowadays, most of us realize that there is a direct link between lifestyle and health. Some people, particularly in the developed world, can afford to make choices about food but still fail to eat a healthy diet. For instance, those who eat a lot of fatty foods often develop high cholesterol that makes them more susceptible to heart disease. At the other end of the scale, children who do not have enough to eat in the poorer countries develop diseases like kwashiorkor (which is directly related to a lack of protein and other nutrients). So why do people who can afford to eat well not choose to live more healthily? And how much can any government or health organization do to influence the choices individuals make about their own health?

Many people cannot afford to buy the ideal daily mix of proteins, carbohydrates, fresh fruits and vegetables, and the nutritional benefits of their diet are therefore limited. In the developing world, many children rarely receive even the bare minimum of food. Even in the developed world, there are significant differences between nutrient intake in different places. For example, people in Mediterranean countries, such as Italy and Greece, benefit from a diet rich in fresh food and olive oil.

Facing up to the risks of smoking

Our increased awareness of how our lifestyle affects our health should make us think more about others. But, unfortunately, not everyone does. We know that passive smoking affects the health of non-smokers. This has been recognized throughout North America where smoking is rarely allowed in public places. Smoking directly affects people's health, as tobacco products contain tar that gathers in the lungs and there is a well-established link between smoking and lung cancer.

FACT

Parts of Scotland have the highest incidence of heart disease, cancer and strokes, the worst tooth decay and the lowest life expectancy in the developed world. The deep-fried Mars Bar is thought to have originated in the north-east of Scotland.

Despite the known health risks, a high proportion of new smokers are young women.

Scientific researchers discovered this link in 1951 and medical authorities in the UK and the US acknowledged it in 1962. Despite long resistance, tobacco companies are now having to acknowledge it too. In the USA in 2001, a man who developed lung cancer in the 1960s was awarded a $100 million compensation payment from a major tobacco company on the grounds that, at that time, there were no clear health warnings on cigarette packets.

DEBATE

In the developed world, obesity, heart disease and alcoholism are an enormous drain on health resources. Do we have the right to literally eat and drink ourselves to death?

An example of extreme deprivation, this malnourished refugee child in Malawi suffers a whole range of health problems.

Developing a healthier world

In 1978, the World Health Assembly resolved to ensure that, by the year 2000, all people of the world would attain a level of health that would permit them to lead socially and economically productive lives. At the G8 Summit in Japan, in 2000, the richest nations of the world recommended the creation of global health funds which would purchase key health products, such as drugs, bed-nets (to guard against malaria-carrying mosquitoes) and vaccines, specially designed for poor countries. Food security (making nutritious food available and affordable) is another key target in developing a healthier world.

Rich health, poor health

General social development through education and literacy usually leads to improved health due to better awareness of nutrition, reproductive health and hygiene. Economic development means better employment, housing and availability of food. In these ways the classic cycle of poverty can be broken by development.

Studies in a range of countries, from Canada and France to South Africa and Brazil, have shown a clear link between social and economic status and health. Put simply, high social status and financial security equal good health, while deprivation results in ill-health. Essentially, deprivation means lack of money, education and opportunity. Development can offer health benefits for the more deprived sections of societies, but in the poorer countries of the world the benefits rarely reach them due to problems of debt, distribution, and lack of transport and communications.

Does development equal good health?

There is some debate about how effective development is in ensuring improved health.

FACT

In 2001, an Indian drugs company Cipla offered to sell a generic three-drug AIDS cocktail to developing countries for $350-600 per patient per year, instead of the $10,000-15,000 charged for the patent protected version in industrialized countries.

Brazilian slum-dwellers. Poor health continues to be linked to poor housing and overcrowding.

The WHO has stated that 'Primary Healthcare is a key part both of a country's health system and of overall economic and social development, without which it is bound to fail. It has to be coordinated on a national basis with the rest of the health system as well as with the other sectors that contribute to a country's total development strategy.'

As so many of the causes of poor health are associated with under-development, it is often argued that policies promoting development will benefit the health of a population. More money generally means more money for health. Yet development can also have negative effects. For example, increased industrialization means more pollution, more dangerous workplaces and a greater dependence on medicines.

VIEWPOINT

'I believe it is important to recognize that hunger deserves at least the same attention as poverty when we look at global development priorities. And sadly, at the dawn of the third millennium, we are still far from ensuring that all people on the planet have enough to eat, when and where they need it.'
Jacques Diouf. Director-General. Food and Agricultural Organization. Italy

*Live Aid Concert, London, 1985.
The Live Aid initiative raised
around $100 million to fight
famine and improve health in
Ethiopia and Somalia.*

Applying band aids

The twenty-first century is an age of instant
information. As soon as a flood or earthquake
occurs anywhere in the world, we see live news
coverage on our televisions. This has made us far
more aware of world health issues than previous
generations, and this awareness means that we are
often very eager to help victims of famines, wars,
disease and natural disasters in other countries.

For example, in 1985 there was a huge response
from the developed world to the specific problems
of starvation and malnutrition linked to famine in
Ethiopia. A number of musicians released a single
('Do They Know It's Christmas?) and the Live Aid
rock concert, organized by Sir Bob Geldof, was
broadcast all over the world, to raise money for
famine relief. When appealed to in this way, the
healthier world showed its willingness to support
people in less healthy parts of the world, and large
amounts of money were donated. But, despite the
success of such appeals, they only provide short-
term relief.

Social exclusion and health

All over the world, ethnic and immigrant groups have less power, and are more deprived and therefore less healthy, than the dominant groups in their societies. These inequalities can be seen in many aboriginal groups, including First Nation (in the USA), Inuits (in North America and Canada), Aboriginals (in Australia) and Romany people (in European countries). Immigrant groups, such as African-Caribbean and Asian communities in the Northern Hemisphere and migrant workers in Southern Africa, also have poorer than average health.

Governments need to ensure that all these inequalities are reduced. In the US, Native Indian Reservations receive special health services to solve immediate problems such as high rates of drug and alcohol addiction. The provision of good general education and health education is also essential.

> ## FACT
>
> In 2000, the WHO estimated that the Roma Gypsy population in Hungary had a life expectancy ten years lower than the rest of the country.

Many Aboriginals suffer from alcoholism, partly linked to their excluded position in Australian society.

Creating a healthier world

Practical intervention can bring results. For instance, blinding malnutrition (xerophthalmia/keratomalacia) is the leading cause of childhood blindness in the world. Each year approximately 500,000 children, mainly in South Asia, go blind, 70 per cent of those due to vitamin A deficiency. The WHO has organized various preventive programmes to combat this problem, distributing vitamin A to infants and children in the worst-affected areas, and helping their families change their diet in order to increase their daily intake of vitamin A.

> ## VIEWPOINT
>
> '"Health for All" does not mean an end to disease and disability, or that doctors and nurses will care for everyone. It means that resources for health are evenly distributed and that essential healthcare is accessible to everyone.'
> *WHO*

THE FUTURE OF WORLD HEALTH

New diseases, new threats

VIEWPOINTS

'Legionnaire's disease is an illness which we have managed to create for ourselves. In designing and constructing systems to control our environment, we have created conditions which can be ideal for the propagation of *Legionella*. Those systems must be properly monitored and maintained. That is the key to controlling this disease.'
John Rimington, Director-General, UK Health and Safety Executive

'Nothing new has happened. Plagues are as certain as death and taxes'
Dr Richard Krause, US National Institutes of Health, discussing why we have so many new infectious diseases

As medical professionals discover more, the human race gets better at understanding the causes of disease. This knowledge helps us find ways of lessening the effects of illnesses. But the stresses and strains of modern life also mean that new health problems keep replacing the old ones. For example, legionnaire's disease was first discovered in Philadelphia in 1976, when twenty-nine people were killed by a bacteria (*Legionella pneumophila*) which spread through the cooling tower of an air-conditioning system.

Every period brings with it the arrival of frightening new diseases. One example is ebola virus, which first appeared in Central Africa in the 1970s. Ebola virus is extremely contagious and very dangerous; the virus gets into the body and eats away many of the internal organs, quickly causing death. An outbreak in Southern Sudan in 1976 saw more than 150 patients die rapidly. A few months later, there was a similar outbreak in the Democratic Republic of Congo. Fortunately, no infected patients were moved to the city of Kinshasa where the disease might have spread to a far greater number of people.

How do new diseases spread?
Migration is a key element in the spread of disease. For example, HIV/AIDS may have existed in Africa for a number of years before spreading to other countries. It has been suggested that greater

migration of people and the multiple use of needles in WHO smallpox vaccination programmes may, ironically, have helped spread the virus.

One way in which new diseases sometimes occur is through cross-species infection. Examples of diseases passed from animals to humans include vCJD (the human form of BSE, known as 'mad cow disease') and a chicken flu virus outbreak in Hong Kong in 1997. These types of disease are particularly dangerous because the human immune system is very different from that of other animals, and we have no defence against them. Whether the source is a virus, bacteria or parasite, it is vital for medical experts to identify it quickly.

FACT

In the US, in 1999, there was an outbreak of a mosquito-based disease called West Nile Virus or Fever. In August and September there were sixty-two cases and seven deaths in New York City.

FACT

An outbreak of ebola virus was reported in Uganda in October 2000. It killed 224 people in two months. About 1,500 cases, with over 1,000 deaths, have been documented since the virus was discovered in 1976.

Hong Kong chickens being taken off for slaughter after an outbreak of so-called 'chicken flu' in 1997.

A genetic future?

A number of other health issues are currently causing a great deal of concern, particularly in the field of genetics. For example, it is now easier for doctors to identify genetic disorders in unborn babies. But this raises difficult questions. Once the mother knows that the foetus has a genetic disorder, such as Down's syndrome or cystic fibrosis, will she be justified in terminating the pregnancy? What about a baby who will be only slightly disabled? Should he or she be given a chance of life?

Dolly, the first ever cloned sheep, symbol of genetic engineering. Will genetic engineering improve or damage human health in the future?

Another issue causing public concern is the long-term impact of genetically modified (GM) foods. The main advantages of GM crops are that they grow quickly, sometimes contain extra nutrients, and are resistant to damage from insects and weeds. This means that they require less herbicide and pesticide and can feed more people, more quickly and cheaply. So, what's the problem? For many people living in poverty in the developing world, GM crops represent a real chance to expand food supply and improve public health.

However, opponents point out that GM crops can pollinate other non-GM crops nearby, which could lead to the evolution of weeds and pests that are resistant to herbicides and pesticides. They are also concerned about the unknown long-term effects of eating genetically mutated foods which could

produce harmful toxins and new allergens. More research still needs to be done, to find out how much substance there is to these fears.

Protestors damaging GM oilseed rape crops at farm trials in the UK.

The plague of war

The focus on disease tends to hide the fact that hundreds of thousands of people die each year in wars and accidents. The search for world peace goes alongside the search for world health. In 1999, over 9 per cent of the world's deaths were caused by accidents, suicides, murders and war.

Wars and the aftermath of wars will continue to be significant killers. In Angola, Cambodia and Mozambique the land mines left buried by armies kill or maim around 15,000 people (including many children) each year. Meanwhile, deaths caused by road traffic accidents have reached staggering proportions. In 2001, road traffic injuries ranked ninth among the leading causes of ill-health and accounted for 2.8 per cent of all global deaths and disability.

FACT

Murder (or homicide) is also a growing problem around the world. In the US, homicide is the second leading cause of death for Americans aged fifteen to thirty-four, and the leading cause of death for African-Americans.

The good news

There are some grounds for optimism. The twentieth century witnessed greater gains in health than at any other time in history. These gains have been partly due to improvements in income, education and nutrition, and access to contraceptives, hygiene, housing, water supplies and sanitation. They have also been due to new knowledge about the causes, prevention and treatment of disease.

A health education session at a street clinic in India.

Many organizations have helped improve world health through prevention and vaccination programmes. They have also helped those who have suffered the effects of natural disasters, such as earthquakes in Turkey and India or floods in Mozambique.

A saner, calmer world?

Mental illness is likely to be a major source of ill-health in the twenty-first century. Although there is a link between stress and mental illness, there are many other factors involved as well, including genetics, physiology, trauma and living conditions. According to the WHO, mental illness now accounts for 11 per cent of the global burden of disease, second only to infectious diseases.

In an increasingly busy world, stress can make people ill. Long working hours, the need to be more profitable and efficient, family breakdown, and lack of exercise all contribute to disease, particularly heart disease, cancer, intestinal problems and mental illness. These stresses are even greater in the developing world, where making a living and staying healthy is even more difficult.

WHO needs help most?

It is often argued that the developed world should take a greater role in improving the health of the developing world. But, because of weaknesses in the health systems in low-income countries, such programmes often fail to reach the poor. One way to improve world health in the long term is to target specific groups who are most in need of help. These include the poor, women, children and young people, refugees and the elderly.

People will always be born, get ill, be cured or die. But it is up to us all to make our own health, and the health of our friends and families, as good and as lasting as possible. To do this for our fellow citizens of the world, no matter where they live, continues to be one of our greatest challenges for the future.

GLOSSARY

acupuncture the science of puncturing the skin with needles at particular points on the body in order to cure illness or relieve pain.

AIDS Acquired Immune Deficiency Syndrome; a condition brought about by Human Immunodeficiency Virus (HIV) which leaves the sufferer very vulnerable to infection, usually leading to death.

allergen something that causes a painful reaction in some people, when it is eaten or breathed in.

antibiotics medicines produced by or made from a micro-organism and able to stop or kill another micro-organism; used to treat serious infections.

carbohydrates substances such as sugars and starches which provide much of the energy in our diet.

complementary and alternative medicine general title for non-conventional approaches to health, e.g. acupuncture and homeopathy.

deprivation suffering from hardship, especially the lack of good education, housing and healthcare.

developed countries generally wealthier countries of the world, including those of Europe and North America, Japan and Australia and New Zealand. People living there usually benefit from good health and education, and work in a variety of service and high-technology industries.

developing countries generally poorer countries of the world, sometimes called the Third World and including most of Africa, Asia, Latin America and Oceania. People living there often suffer poor health and education, and work in agriculture and lower-technology industries.

disease ecology the scientific study of the evolution and spread of disease in relation to the pathogen, host and the environment in which the disease develops.

disease incidence the number of new cases of a disease found in a given area in a given time period, e.g. a year.

disease prevalence the total number of cases of a disease in a given population at a certain point in time, e.g. on a specific date.

disease severity either the amount of disability caused by the disease or the proportion of all cases of a disease that result in death.

dysentery a very severe form of diarrhoea, usually caused by an infection.

epidemic a disease that spreads quickly, affecting a large proportion of the population.

epidemiology the science of diseases and epidemics, how they occur, how many people they affect, and how badly they affect them.

GDP Gross Domestic Product, the total value of services produced by a nation in a particular year.

generic drugs cheaper, non-patent-protected drugs.

genetic engineering the manipulation of the genes that make up all living things. Used to produce GM crops and foodstuffs.

GM foods foodstuffs that have had their genes changed (genetically modified – GM) in order to improve their productivity.

haemophilia a hereditary illness affecting males; it slows down blood-clotting and makes it difficult to stop the blood flowing, even in cases of minor injuries and cuts; sufferers may need frequent blood transfusions.

HIV Human Immunodeficiency Virus; a virus which destroys the body's immune system and its ability to combat disease and illness.

homeopathy a system of treating diseases by giving minute quantities of drugs that trigger symptoms similar to those of the disease.

immunization see vaccination.

indigenous people people who come from a

particular place.

kwashiorkor severe malnutrition in infants and children, caused by lack of protein in their diet.

morbidity rate the incidence of illness, disease or poor health in a population (as opposed to the mortality rate).

mortality rate the frequency or number of deaths in a population.

negligence failure to act in a careful manner when carrying out normal duties; 'medical negligence' refers to medical staff who cause harm to patients when treating them.

patent the right of a particular individual or company to control the sale and distribution of a product which they have invented or developed.

pathogens germs and viruses which cause disease.

primary care healthcare provided outside hospitals to people living in the community, generally through GPs, home visit nurses, local health centres and clinics.

public health the health of a community, maintained by means of sanitation, good hygiene practices, etc.

re-hydration solution salts and sugar which, when mixed with water, help restore essential fluids to the body; especially important when bodily fluids are lost through illnesses causing diarrhoea.

vaccination injecting a person with a mild form of a germ or virus in order to give them immunity to the disease.

viruses infectious agents which are smaller than bacteria and which multiply only within living cells; they are responsible for a wide range of infectious diseases including measles and influenza.

BOOKS TO READ

The Story of the New Genetics
J.S. Kidd and R.A. Kidd
(Facts on File, 1999)

**The Development of Medicine
for OCR GCSE**
Colin Shepherd
(Hodder & Stoughton, 2002)

Teach Yourself Instant Reference: Medicine
Helicon (Hodder & Stoughton, 2001)

Epidemic
Eyewitness Guide
Brian Ward
(Dorling Kindersley, 2001)

Medicine
Eyewitness Guide
Steve Parker
(Dorling Kindersley, 2000)

Earth Strikes Back: Water
Arthur Haswell
(Belitha Press, 2000)

USEFUL ADDRESSES

http://www.who.int/home-page/
http://www.who.int/whosis/ (statistics)
World Health Organization: The key source of world health information. This site has links by country, disease and other topics. It also has a series of fact sheets on different world health issues and on policies aimed at bringing about equality in world health. The site also includes the most recent World Health Reports.

http://www.cdc.gov/
http://www.cdc.gov/health/diseases.htm
CDC: A US government site run by the Center for Disease Control with lots of information about specific diseases in the US.

http://mole.utsa.edu/~matserv/iheal/
IHEAL: This site specializes in environmental health issues. The IHEAL Directory of Health & Environment Links is a portal to hundreds of electronic databases and information resources.

http://healthatoz.com/atoz/default.asp
Health A to Z: An excellent general family health site with lots of information about different aspects of diet, lifestyle and general health promotion issues. Also has some good interactive tools to allow you to assess the state of your own health.

http://www.healthnet.org.uk/
Healthnet: A magazine-style format with an emphasis on health education made fun and entertaining. Features fact sheets on diet, exercise and smoking.

http://www.biozone.co.uk/HEALTH_AND_D
ISEASE.html
Biozone: An excellent educational website with a whole series of links to relevant sites based around some of the key themes of this book, including diseases, diet and the body.

World Health Organization
Avenue Appia 201211
Geneva 27
Switzerland
Tel: +00 41 22 791 21 11

Center for Disease Control (US)
CDC Washington Office
200 Independence Avenue, SW
Room 746G
Washington DC 20201
Tel: +00 1 202 690 8598

Department of Health (UK)
The Department of Health
Richmond House
79 Whitehall
London SW1A 2NS
Tel: 0207 210 4850

BIOZONE Learning Media (UK) Ltd
P.O. Box 16710
Glasgow G12 9WS
Scotland
Tel: 0141 337 3355

INDEX

Numbers in **bold** refer to illustrations.